THE DAY I MET REIKI

Anne Williams
Reiki Master 3a and Holy Fire 111 Reiki Ryoho Reiki Master Teacher

Published by New Generation Publishing in 2022

Copyright © Anne Williams 2022

First Edition

The author asserts the moral right under the Copyright, Designs and Patents Act 1988 to be identified as the author of this work.

All Rights reserved. No part of this publication may be reproduced, stored in a retrieval system or transmitted, in any form or by any means without the prior consent of the author, nor be otherwise circulated in any form of binding or cover other than that which it is published and without a similar condition being imposed on the subsequent purchaser.

ISBN   978-1-80369-442-9

www.newgeneration-publishing.com
New Generation Publishing

I would like to dedicate this book to my brother, Terence Ratcliffe, who sadly passed away on the 21st April 2020.

Acknowledgements

My gratitude and thanks to my eldest daughter, Sarah, who taught me Reiki. Thank you for spending so many hours patiently showing me how to use Reiki and teaching me Reiki 1 and 11.

Thanks to Karla, my youngest daughter and Howard, my husband, for modelling for my couch treatment photos.

To Andrea, my teacher who taught me Reiki Master Usui on 5th July 2014 and Reiki Master Usui Holy Fire 11 Reiki Ryoho on the 12th June 2016.

And thanks to the International Center for the Holy Fire 111 Reiki Master teacher upgrade signed certificate given to me on the 11th January, 2019 by the president William Lee Rand .

CHAPTER 1

I had known about Reiki for many years and had been around Reiki for most of my years as I watched my daughter speak about and do Reiki. She would always tell me about it so it seemed I was learning more about it bit by bit but not really understanding Reiki. Every time I saw my daughter she would be talking about it. Eventually, a few months later, I attended a workshop with two Masters taking the class; I also invited a small group of friends as they seemed to be very interested, plus I thought safety in numbers! When the day arrived we all met in my house, I converted my dining room into a Reiki treatment room with a make shift bed for a massage table, candles and chairs so we could all eagerly listen. My friends were all excited as I got all of us a drink and some cake, biscuits, some fruit and snacks. Eventually the class began. The Masters took it in turns explaining how Reiki was rediscovered by Dr

Mikao Usui in Japan, where Dr Usui climbed the sacred mountain Mount Kuri Yama outside Kyoto, and chose a special place to meditate. According to the story he faces east and collected 21 stones so that he could remain aware of how many days he spent there by throwing away a stone a day. For 20 days he meditated and felt nothing but on the 21st day of meditating Dr Usui prayed to seek for enlightenment and a sign, whilst praying he saw a light appear in the darkness, which grew in size as it approached him. He began to feel very frightened and wondered what he had prayed for but stayed to see if this light would finally give him what he prayed for.

The light got closer to him until it landed on the middle of his forehead, completely and utterly bewildered he next saw millions of coloured bubbles. The bubbles slowly turned into white bubbles with each one containing a Reiki symbol in gold that he had discovered in the Tibetan scripts. One by one the bubbles appeared one at a time. He studied each sign before it disappeared. He was given the meaning of each one and how it could be used to energize healing energy when performing a Reiki treatment. People say this was the first miracle. When he collected his thoughts he found it was daylight so he started walking down the mountain quickly, eagerly hoping to tell his friends what had happened, but he fell over a stone and badly cut his toe. He bent down to touch his cut toe and to his amazement a few minutes later he healed his toe, it stopped bleeding and the pain was better, his healing seemed to have taken place. That was the second miracle.

Coming further down the mountain Dr Usui stopped at an Inn for a drink and something to eat; he must have been very hungry after meditating for 21 days without food. After such a long fast the owner of the Inn advised him to eat a light meal. Dr Usui didn't listen and ordered a large Japanese breakfast and ate it very quickly and to his surprise didn't have any indigestion or pain. Whilst eating he noticed a young girl at the Inn who was the granddaughter of the owner of the Inn, she had a swollen jaw and was in pain with her teeth. Dr Usui asked if he could help her pain and put his hand on her jaw; to his surprise the pain stopped and the swelling went down. This was the third miracle.

After this exciting day Dr Usui carried on walking back to Zen monastery and met up with the abbot who suffered from arthritis; he once again put his hands on the painful area and the pain disappeared. This was the fourth miracle.

The next day Dr Usui discussed with the abbot how he could help others, so he went out onto the streets to work with the beggars of Kyoto, to help them with their suffering. He left his monastery which had been his home and decided to live with the beggars for several years, healing them and trying to get them to change their way of life. But after a few years Dr Usui realised they were not going to change their ways and carried on begging, this upset him greatly and he realised that although he had healed the body, he had not healed the spirit as the monks had told him. Dr Usui realised exchange of energy was vital as people needed to give something back for the healing they had received.

Dr Usui left the beggars quarters and decided to use the symbols that he had been given and taught Reiki healing throughout Japan. Teaching people how to treat themselves. Dr Usui created five spiritual principles, after working with the beggars in Japan he realised his healing was not appreciated and people were not taking responsibility for their lives. The principles were designed around appreciating life and how to grow and take charge of your own life.

The five Spiritual principles are:
    Just for today do not worry.
    Just for today do not anger.
    Honour your parents, teachers and elders. Earn

your living honestly.

Show gratitude to every living thing.

These are wise words Dr Mikao Usui.

During our Reiki share evening the Reiki Masters explained how Reiki share is about a fair exchange of energy and goodwill, so everyone there had to contribute, my dear friend Diane brought along a delicious chocolate cake homemade which we all enjoyed! After this we all had the opportunity to have a hands on go at Reiki. That was my first experience of Reiki. Wow! I had one Master on my head and the other on my stomach area, it was amazing as the Master told me afterwards that she could see an orange colour. A year later I ended up having a keyhole operation for a hernia in that area, and even though the Reiki healing didn't heal the hernia it warned me to do something about it before it got worse. Everyone else had a go with hands on Reiki and we all had lots of fun experiencing the treatment. Afterwards we all had a drink of water to clear the imbalances from the body.

So that was where my interest in Reiki began for me, but it wasn't until sometime later that I was approached by a Reiki Master to train. I was in London, in a beautiful pub, sitting on a stool by the bar having a glass of wine with my daughter Sarah, her husband and my hubby, Sarah took my hand and looked me in the eyes and said, "Mum, you really should learn, you would be very good at Reiki, your energies are perfect."

"Are they," I replied.

I was a bit shocked! "Learn Reiki. I don't think I could do that I don't think I'm special enough for the responsibility of healing people." But she insisted I would be.

Later on, I got together with Sarah and started training with her, I took to the training like a duck to water, I couldn't learn fast enough. I wanted to learn more and more. She explained how the energies felt and how you feel giving Reiki healing, how we channel our pure energy to the client. She taught me how to let Reiki guide you and your hands will find it.

I started practising on my friends and family and gradually my confidence increased; I felt stronger somehow, I was changing for the better, I was more aware of life rather than letting things pass me by. My path was clear, I was connecting in a wonderful new life of wonder and all the spiritual things that was going to happen to me. Masters say Reiki comes to people when they are ready, well there you go! I had the taste of Reiki and it felt marvellous, overwhelming somewhat, but I needed to know more.

I learnt how our body works. The chakras in our bodies are like a wheel are located in seven major points on the aura. The chakras are like spiritual energy centres spin at a slow, normal or fast speed, this tells me how the body is functioning properly. To move through the body via the chakras moving my hands gently over my client's body or hovering my hands gently.

I found out the meaning of heat how it heals and how to correct the imbalances the more I worked with Reiki and the chakras the colours of the spinning rotation, it seemed to be very clear to me. A great guide to how I work with even today.

I never get fed up with Reiki it seems part of me now, how I look at people, wanting to help them flow through the universe with ease, happiness and positivity.

When I was training I found information on

how to work with heat here are examples.

Heat: Needs more Reiki energy in this area. Can indicate a physical problem

Coolness: Might be an emotional problem. Also the Chakra may not be working well.

Tingling: Can be withheld anger.

Dull pain: An old injury an area where a scar might need extra treatment.

Sharp pain: Too much energy in the aura causing an imbalance. Needs more Reiki to release the energy.

I once treated a client years ago, I found a really dull pain in his leg it surprised me and after his treatment I asked him what it was, he told me "in the war he was injured with shrapnel pieces shot in his leg" that was fifty years ago. Amazing how Reiki picks things up.

Reiki does find imbalances in the body from years ago, I have realised this as I do more treatments i.e. like my client with the shrapnel pieces in his leg which was causing him pain. By giving him Reiki in this area of his leg it balanced it. You never stop learning about Reiki.

The more Reiki's you do your energies get stronger, it is fascinating how each client is different. Also by giving a Reiki, I receive one back. People often ask me do I get tired, physically and mentally, no I answer I do not. If you stand properly and balance and connect to Reiki I have always been ok. Making sure you ground yourself properly and protect yourself from unwanted energies before they come also a little Reiki prayer, when I begin Reiki treatment, or, if they are new to Reiki I say my prayer out loud so they can hear me so they know what's going on.

My prayer I always say this to myself is:

"Turn the outcome of this energy to the highest good".

Namaste

CHAPTER 2

Training for Reiki 1

I started my training in London where my daughter Sarah lived; she lived in a very pretty house with plenty of character. She always met me at the station and it was always so good to see her and her little dog Jessie. When we got to her house we would just sit and chat and very calmly talk about Reiki, how to adjust to one's energy levels, how to ground yourself every day to keep your energies centred (to this day I still do grounding exercises every day, it's funny how habits stick isn't it!). Sarah would tell me of the experiences that had happened to her at home, one of them was how headless spirits would follow her about in her London home. I must admit I was a bit shocked and asked her, "Are you alright with that?"

"Oh! Yes Mum," she said, "they are harmless and it's quite nice really."

Something was definitely changing inside me, I

felt an overwhelming sense of happiness and couldn't stop smiling at life, laugh, if you may but that's how I felt. It felt as if I was having a complete wash out from the inside. I would travel home on the train after saying bye to Sarah and I really felt so happy. We would meet regularly and talk about the next phase in my Reiki training. One day I was standing on my patio in my back garden looking at our fishpond and I suddenly realised how green in colour our grass was and how pretty my roses looked, so definite in colour. At this stage I also started meditating, I had a large yellow flower windmill that you can buy for children on the beach, I put it at the end of my garden and started meditating, concentrating on the flower with its smiley face and each day I centered my thoughts on my windmill. I later found out that I was meditating using creative visualisation, it's a wonderful way to learn, I often help clients today that come to me for treatments. I also noticed that people were becoming more attracted to me, I suppose my energies were changing and I was becoming popular, it's kind of like when you feel really happy, people sense this don't they and they also want to join in.

I managed to decorate a small room in my house to start my Reiki treatment. I bought a new carpet, massage table, candles and Reiki music, the result was amazing! It's nice to have a room especially for Reiki treatments, but not essential as I have practised on friends in their own homes, that's the beauty of Reiki it's a first aid tool you can use it anywhere, your hands do the healing, follow your hands and Reiki will find where to go.

I was shown the basic hand positions in Reiki and how we concentrate and check the chakras for any blockages and how to release them and how to protect ourselves from unwelcome energies. During a treatment my hands may experience different experiences that I do not fully comprehend, it felt pretty weird at first but I quickly got used to it as I practised on my friends.

I also used to Reiki my house, it's a bit like a spring clean but clearing the energies of each room; my plants also loved Reiki, they would almost beg for it, and my cat Pip, who was actually my youngest daughter's cat who we were looking after whilst she was at university, seemed to love Reiki for a few minutes and would then go away when he'd had enough. Oh yes, animals love Reiki, my daughter Sarah has a beautiful horse she has had since he was a foal, Bailey, and she has used Reiki treatments on him for years.

The months went by and I carried on with my Reiki, then one day Sarah said to me that she would like to visit and see my Reiki room. We had a wonderful day together, but unfortunately, she told me I wasn't ready to train for Reiki 2 as I wasn't as balanced as she would have liked me to be. It takes time for all this to change balance itself out within your body and I felt sad that I couldn't go further with my Reiki at this time. I didn't give up though, I was still as positive as I could be and thought to myself it will happen when I am ready. Then one day my daughter asked how I was feeling, I told her I am just fine. She then asked how was I getting on with my Reiki, "Yes good," I said, and I suddenly realised I wasn't as worried about things it was really just a matter-of-fact thing and I was accepting it. When I told my daughter this she said, "That's it, you are balanced, you're ready for Reiki 2."

That was the icing on the cake for me, I couldn't believe it, I was jumping for joy!

Before my Reiki 1 attunement, just like Dr Usui did 21 days on the mountain, I was asked to Reiki myself for 21 days every day, with no alcohol and having a light diet, it takes discipline, but I did it, actually I lost a bit of weight as well.

My attunement for Reiki 1 was a wonderful experience. I stayed with my daughter for the weekend.

I received my Masters attunements, I felt great symbols directed on my head area. My head felt heavy and light all at once. Afterwards we sat chatting about how I felt, I drank a glass of water relaxed and pondered about my attunement. We then went out for dinner. I watched Sarah blessing her food pasta and plant dishes, that is when I decided to eat more plant based food it is better for you, I gave up meat and started cooking in tofu, coconut oil and drinking no dairy products, I changed my way of eating and drinking milk. I like coffee so I have decaf at home occasionally I might have a coffee at the coffee shop they smell lush!! Maybe a cake naughty! I haven't eaten meat for about fifteen years now, I do feel better for it. When we came back from dinner we went to bed. I slept really well I remember feeling happy and content ready for a new day.

I bought myself some pure oils to use. Started burning different ones. I love the fragrance of rose oil I have a rose quartz crystal, which I am very fond of so they compliment each other. Getting myself ready for treatments. It was so much fun buying myself a uniform in white with my name embroidered on it. That's the thing, nice to look the part professional when your clients arrive it is important to give that impression. I waited 6 months to a year before I embarked on Reiki 2 in Reiki it is needed for your energies to settle. I did Reiki's on my friends and family for free to get the practise and it worked everything was falling into place. I was so eager to move on to Reiki 2. When the day arrived it was so exciting I couldn't believe it. I am moving on, I know it is silly but it meant the world to me. Then the day arrived..........

CHAPTER 3

Training for Reiki 2

Reiki 2 training is completely different to Reiki 1, it's more advanced and a real commitment. When you have completed the Reiki 2 training you can start charging for your treatments. Most people are quite happy to stay at Reiki 1 and are happy with that, but I felt I needed to push on with my Reiki 2 and so I did.

Sarah and her husband moved from London to Somerset to a somewhat beautiful village and bought a church and renovated it. This made my training so special and interesting because when the renovations were complete I started to feel the wonderful energies in each of the rooms. One particular night I stayed in one of the bedrooms and I just couldn't sleep, I woke up and felt that the room was very busy with spirit people talking, it wasn't scary, far from it, but it wasn't until the morning that I asked my daughter what this part of the church was before they converted it. Sarah told me it was the vestry. Well, that explained everything. Needless to say, I wasn't too keen on staying in that bedroom again. This spiritual knowledge was my very first opening into the Reiki world, with much more to come. You see my spiritual alignment was growing, I accepted it for what it was, it was quite interesting. Another time I stayed with my daughter, in the same bedroom, during the day, whilst I was in the bedroom, I suddenly had an impression of something pushing against the outer wall, I couldn't explain it, then two weeks later a drunk driver lost control of his truck and smashed into my daughter's front wall almost hitting the house, it could have been very serious indeed. It felt very weird to think I felt something two weeks before it happened. Sarah and I had such fun learning the knowledge of Reiki, I grew to love it very much. I also became quite serious on how I was feeling and how I should cope with my new found knowledge. I learned to use the sacred symbols and memorise them I learnt to meditate and commit to the way I was feeling. Although my daughter and her husband had renovated the church into a lovely home I felt the energies were everywhere, so I asked non-Reiki people to see if they could pick up on this feeling, but they couldn't, so I knew my energies were stronger. There was a peaceful energy to the home, and I actually felt at peace and happy there.

Have you ever walked into a house and felt happy, or the reverse, where you can't wait to get out of there!

A family visitor came to see my daughter and husband who started talking about Reiki with me; it's strange really how all of a sudden I'm wanted and it felt good. Apparently, she was getting divorced; so many of us experience this, including me, which for many years left me feeling worthless, then suddenly my life had a purpose again by helping people and that's exactly what I did. She asked if I would give her a treatment even though I hadn't been attuned in Reiki 2, I could practise on my friends and family. She loved the treatment and thanked me for my help; in return I felt amazing myself and quickly realised that every time I gave a Reiki I received one back.

As I progressed with my Reiki 2 training I began learning more of the sacred symbols; it took a while for me to learn them but I did it in the end. I also love meditating, I do it every day as it clears my thoughts and makes me feel positive and revitalised for the day. You can meditate for 10 minutes or hours, whatever fits into your lifestyle, and you don't have to be sat in weird positions, personally I find it uncomfortable. I like sitting on my favourite chair, this works so long as you switch off your thoughts. I get told time and time again that I can't do that, but with practise it comes to you naturally in the end. Although, when I started meditating I used to stand and watch my garden windmill and do some quick meditation staring out at the windmill, it's what suits you best that matters. I carried on with my training with Sarah and visited her regularly, we had such happy times at her home in Somerset. I quickly recognised how different advanced Reiki 2 was to Reiki 1 and how much of a real commitment it is because once qualified I would be able to set up a business and start charging clients.

My Reiki 2 attunement was very special and something I will never forget. It occurred over a weekend at Sarah's home, in a large room with candles adorning each side of the room and incense burning. In the dimly lit room I sat in a comfortable chair in the prayer position whilst my Master was stood a few feet away in front of me. I closed my eyes whilst she performed the sacred symbols on my head; it felt like there was a heavy feeling but it was not an unpleasant sensation, then when she had finished, she moved away very quietly. I started to cry with happiness, I did feel stupid and told Sarah afterwards, but she told me she had cried at her attunement which made me feel better. It must be the pure intensity of attunements that makes them so emotional. She also told me I had a lot of people from the spirit world who were adorning the room with bright light, and my mother and father, who passed away over 20 years ago, were standing behind me. I felt overwhelmed and happy; Sarah then told me she thought my mother and father were my two guides, which pleased me, and that I was now officially a peoples Reiki practitioner. Some practitioners love healing animals more than humans, which was interesting to know.

After my attunement I bought some pansies and planted them in a pretty stone container in the garden to connect with nature.

A stream at the end of Sarah's garden I walked along the pathway, a gentle breeze, warm and sunny day, a perfect day. I felt total peace within myself to move on with my Reiki, helping people to feel warm inside and happy.

Exciting, how we learn to do things and achieve what we are aiming for and when we fulfil our dreams its special.

CHAPTER 4

The Start of My Reiki Practice

Now all I had to do was find some clients to help and heal. I decided to get some business cards printed and some Reiki leaflets. I put them in my local shops and gave some to my friends and family so they could spread the word. It didn't take long for me to get my first client: I received a call from a gentleman who called himself Peter, when he phoned me, I was so excited to talk to him. With his permission Peter has written a recommendation which you can read below: -

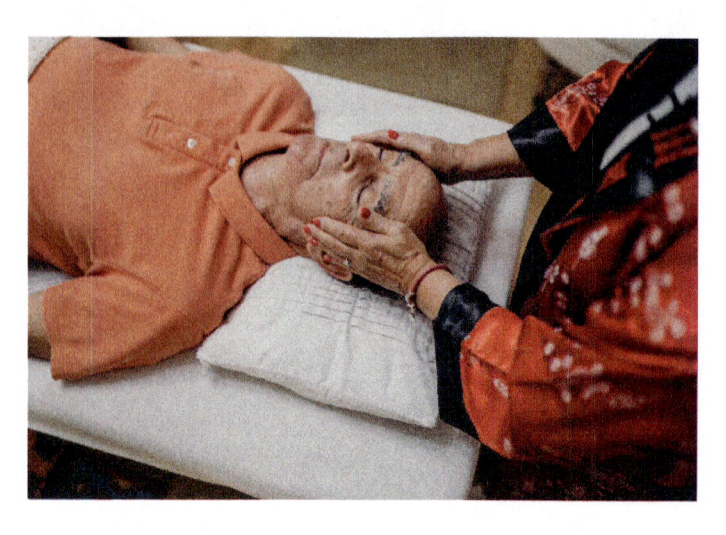

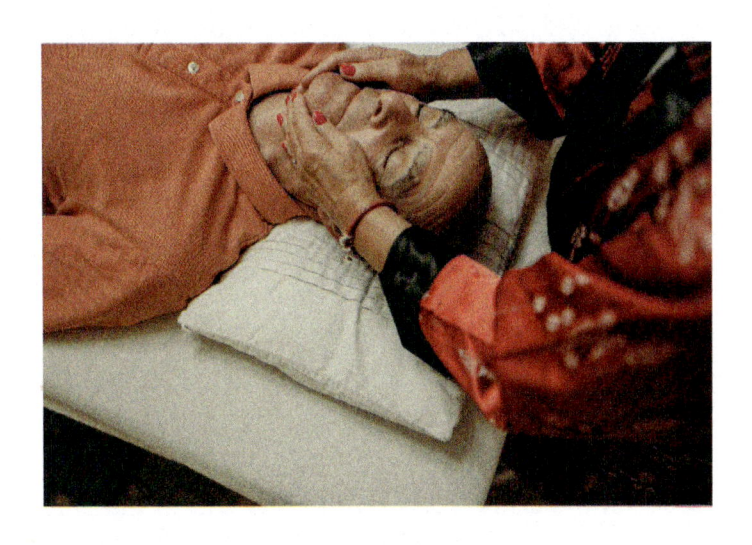

1st June 2010 <u>Without Prejudice</u>
Re REIKI Treatment

I had the privilege and pleasure of receiving REIKI treatment from Mrs Anne Williams over a period of approximately 18 months from December 2007 to August 2009.

During my treatments I found that Mrs Williams had tremendous healing powers combined with a very relaxed, thorough and structured approach to the treatment that I received.

I found REIKI particularly helpful for me and continued my treatments for relaxation purposes, stress relief and well-being.

I would certainly recommend Anne to anyone that requires REIKI healing.

Yours faithfully,

Peter

Peter enjoyed his Reiki treatments and to this day we still keep in touch; he is a very dear friend.

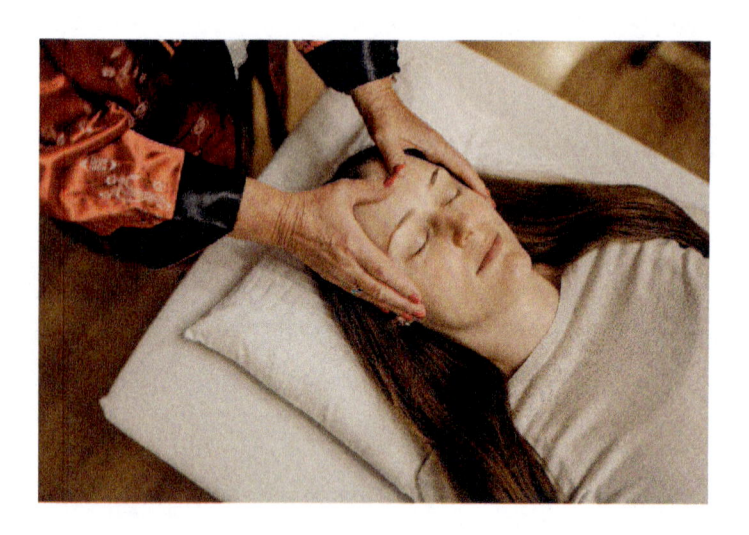

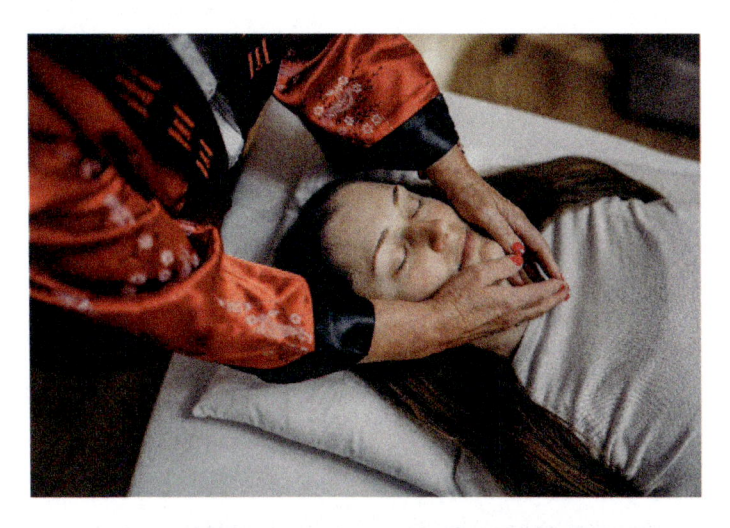

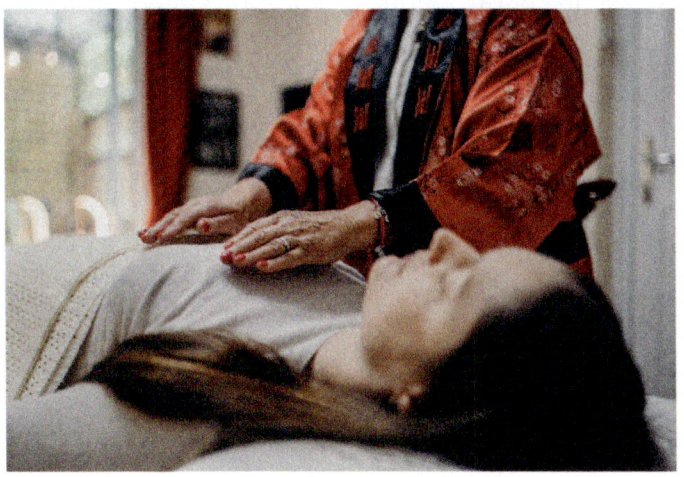

EXPERIENCES IN REIKI TREATMENTS

When preparing for a treatment with my clients at least 35 minutes before they arrive I meditate and pray. I must add that Reiki is suitable for everyone it isn't of any religion, rich or poor, it is a simple way of achieving balance and healing the mind, body and soul, reminding the body what it once had but has since forgotten. When we were in our mother's womb we hadn't experienced harm, hurt or happy emotions, it's only until we enter the big wide world and experience good or bad things that these emotions stay with us. We forget the purity of being a baby, so this is a good way to remind us and refresh our body's energies.

Coming back to my first Reiki session with Peter, we had a good session (in Reiki we channel our pure energy with the client's energy as one). Peter booked weekly Reiki sessions after that and things began to improve week by week, but something just didn't seem right. It was only after a few sessions with him I quickly realised he was suffering from Fibromyalgia. He told me he had been suffering from this illness for over 10 years and would try anything to get relief, or to get better. Some months later he started to climb up my stairs to my treatment room with ease instead of walking painfully like he did when he had started with me. He seemed to be getting some relief from Reiki. He continued to come each week for a long time that is until I moved to Hampshire. We still keep in touch by email, he tells me he is still well, hopefully I will see him again when he visits me in Southampton.

A few weeks later a lady booked some treatments, she was called Debbie, pretty lady in her early 40s, I asked her what she was coming for, trying to get some idea of her treatment. She always spoke with a husky voice and when I gave her first treatment I found her throat chakra wasn't right. I was burning rose oil, which represents unconditional love, and when I started her treatment a lovely elderly lady sat by her side, she was as clear to me as a normal person, looking lovingly at Debbie. That was the very first time I experienced spirits come down in my Reiki treatment room. I asked Debbie after her treatment who this lady was, she said, "Oh! That's my Grandma Rose, she always protects me and comes to me on my birthday, funerals and anything new I do." I was extremely surprised by this. As we progressed further into her treatments there was another surprise in store for me, she explained she wasn't happy with her marriage and her husband had been very hostile to her for many years. I explained to her that is the reason why her throat is husky. After quite a few Reiki treatments, she said she loved coming to me, found it peaceful and she felt safe with me, I quickly realised just how unhappy she really was. Time went on and the months rolled by and then one day she arrived for her usual treatment and told me before we started that she had left her husband, she felt a huge sense of relief and to my astonishment her throat chakra began clearing, she started speaking normally. For 25 years she had suffered with her voice, but now it was perfectly normal.

Reiki had given her the positive energy to get

out of this terrible situation and find peace as well as health.

Debbie kept in touch with me from time to time and I was so happy for her, she told me she had met a really lovely man and she felt she could move on with her life and trust again.

I felt blessed by Reiki, if I can make a difference to one life that was enough for me. As I carried on with Reiki treatments I experienced so many different energies and situations.

One day I had a treatment with a lady who had a terrible back, she had seen my leaflet in the local shop, at the time I didn't think anything of it until she arrived and I could see she was clearly in so much pain. Once again, I let Reiki move my hands to where the energy was needed and trusted. When I checked her back she assured me there were no slipped discs it was just pain, then when I felt her sacrum, the large bone at the bottom of the spine, it was red HOT! There was clearly something wrong so I stayed in this position for a while, it seemed like I was in this one position for 15 minutes, then eventually it cleared and got cooler. I did a full Reiki as well, but I don't know why I turned her over to look at her back, it seemed like the right thing to do, and even to this day I do this now and the amount of clients that come to me who feel hot in this area is alarming, it seems like a lot of bad energy is stored in this area. After her Reiki treatment she started to look a bit better, but I warned her that she might feel quite sore for a few days; her husband even rang me to say she was very ill the next day but I told him this would pass and sure enough on the third day she was up and about hopping about like a spring chicken! Well, not quite like that, but better and she continued her treatments. Her husband was so impressed that even he wanted to book a treatment with me, he also had back problems but he had a slipped disc and I told him he would have to get it put back properly before I could see him and sure enough he did. Then he came to me for a Reiki treatment and the heat on his back was amazing! But after a few days he was fine. I saw him and his wife out a few months later and told me they have never looked back and thanked me.

"Thanks to Reiki," I said.

I was staying at my eldest daughter's home for a short break, one day she asked me to come and see Bailey, her pride and joy. He didn't seem to be very happy which was unusual for Bailey as he was a happy horse at the best of times. Sarah told me he was unwell, and then she performed Reiki on him which was interesting to watch, he seemed to know what was happening, it was lovely. This is the beauty of Reiki it can be used on anything that has energy, it is so natural and pure.

When I was putting my house up for sale I went in each room and energised each room, holding my hands on the walls. I could actually feel the energy radiating through the walls. It didn't take long to sell! Also, my friends and family who have stayed with me have said they felt my house seemed energised and happy.

I had a beautiful plant, a cacti I grew from a couple of leaves, I decided to try to root it and it took, I had that plant for seven years, it grew so big, at least 1ft tall and wide, it was very special to me because when my youngest daughter went to university I missed her so much and this little plant was special as I planted it to remind me of her going to university. When we moved I didn't have the room for this plant so my daughter offered to take it to work as it was cosy and warm in her office and had lots of people to keep it company.

One day they were having a meeting in the same room my cacti was in and it was such a surprise to learn from Karla that Karla's boss and her colleagues saw my poor old cacti literally keel over and die. To this day I wonder if it missed my daily Reiki touch!

Moments in Reiki are very special, with no gain to oneself, selfless and giving so perfectly pure. You get so much back from Reiki, a feeling of love in your heart that is fulfilling and this radiates to other people as they seem to want to talk to you more and love your presence, they are attracted to you like a magnet. It's a good feeling if someone else does something nice for you, a simple act of kindness, like the other day I was walking to open a shop door when a gentleman opened the door for me and tipped his hat, I smiled at him and said thank you. That kind of thing.

There are so many experiences I have had with Reiki but I will try to recall some of them in my book, like the ones I have written about so far. As

I travel with the Reiki experiences of the wonder of the events to happen.

As it usually happens for me most of my Reiki treatments are from recommendations or I chat to people and they ask for a Reiki leaflet and then they phone to book for an appointment.

My husband and I belonged to our local Green Bowling Club, needless to say I think it was more social rather than playing for me, but Howie, my husband, is very good at it, he loves it and he became very popular, I felt very proud of him. We were having afternoon tea at our bowls club when I was approached by a really lovely elderly gentlemen called Norman, he asked me what Reiki was and we had an in-depth chat and he told me he had pains in his back. I asked him to come and have a treatment with me, hopefully Reiki would at least relax him. When he arrived I asked him to wash his hands, that's the first rule of thumb when clients come, and then we had a brief chat as I explained how Reiki works and he settled down on my comfortable massage table. Whilst performing Reiki on his head area it seemed out of balance so I stayed in this position for some time, not knowing that Norman had actually had cancer treatment on his lumps on his head, Reiki had picked this up, he confirmed he had had treatment on his head and was very surprised to find that Reiki found it. His back was definitely sore and Reiki helped with this to. Norman came to me for quite a few treatments, thoroughly enjoying the relaxing feeling of Reiki. Needless to say he wasn't too happy when I said we were moving to Hampshire to move nearer our daughters. I have kept in touch with him and we exchange Christmas cards every year.

Moving to Hampshire seemed quite hard, in one way I wanted so much to live near my daughters, but in another way I felt so sad leaving my Reiki clients, I felt torn and very guilty, Peter still tells me to come back to Southend-on-Sea, we need you. My mind was made up, I had to do what I desired for a change and it did seem right. The months went by and eventually we sold our house to a lovely family, I was so pleased they bought our lovely house with the lovely Reiki energies. My eldest daughter Sarah helped us find a beautiful bungalow in Waterlooville, Portsmouth, we visited it once, it was very pretty detached bungalow with a lovely garden full of fruit trees and a gorgeous little Japanese bridge and decking. I fell in love with it. So we bought it. When the day arrived to get the keys we were so excited, but when we walked in I could feel the bad energy, I felt as though this bungalow doesn't want me here, but I dismissed these thoughts. The kitchen was all pine, 21ft long, overlooking the garden, but I still couldn't get over this feeling of negative feelings. The removal men were so good, they had worked hard all day so I sent my Howie to buy fish and chips for all of us, we all had a laugh amongst all the boxes around us. We all went to bed exhausted and woke up the next morning ready to start unpacking. But again the energy of the house didn't seem right. I thought, oh no, what have I done. But I dismissed it again. We moved into the bungalow in September 2009 and the cracks soon appeared in this pretty little bungalow, it needed a lot of work, we ended up spending roughly £15,000 on the property, but the money wasn't what bothered me, it was this feeling of bad energy. I joined the swimming pool down the road and as soon as I closed the door on the bungalow it was as if a cloud had lifted, I couldn't work it out as I hadn't lived in such an evil place before.

Christmas came, which was a quiet family celebration, and was very nice. But I noticed that Karla's boyfriend Lee didn't feel well and asked him what was wrong. He told me he didn't feel well and asked me if I could give him a Reiki treatment. When I gave Lee a Reiki treatment I felt a physical imbalance in his heart and kidneys. I told Lee to go to the doctors, he did and his doctor gave him a blood test, three weeks later it was confirmed that Lee had cancer, they started treatment straight away, they were brilliant. Lee was only 22 years old at the time and we were all very sad. He was very brave, he asked if he could sometimes stay with us and with his Mum, I was so worried when I would hear him being sick after every treatment. As the months went by the chemotherapy finished and was successful. We were so relieved and Lee was slowly recovering.

Then one day Karla told me she couldn't get up in the night to go to the toilet and said she was frightened; that wasn't like Karla, she is normally very brave. As we carried on living at the bungalow life got much worse, the place was definitely not right. Then evil struck again. At the end of April, I was swimming and when I was in the changing rooms I found a lump on my left breast, I froze, no it can't be! Anyway, I was doing a Reiki treatment and I knew then it was cancer. I went to the doctors and she told me that there is definitely a lump but you have just had a mammogram done and your results were normal so don't worry about it, but she did advise that maybe I should go to the hospital and get it checked out. Two weeks later I had a biopsy, then one week later I was told it was cancer. I instantly thought that I was going to die, I cried and called for Howie; the nurses were fantastic and took me through the treatment one step at a time. I had to have chemotherapy after surgery and I got through all that. I felt very calm in the hospital but, as I came home I found the house overwhelming, it was as if the place was choking me. That night I woke up and felt as though there was this dark thing over my head, I thought it was going to suffocate me. My husband's business collapsed shortly after, he had no money, so we had to sell this place as quickly as we could. I instructed the local Estate Agent to come in and deal with it, he was marvellous and sold the place to a cash buyer within a few months, I couldn't get out of this bungalow fast enough. To this day I still wonder if that place was built on bad ground so the bad energies were still there. Before we left, I said goodbye to both my neighbours as both sides were detached bungalows, there was three in a row, and we were in the middle, and sure enough one of my neighbours told me that they wake up to the smell of cakes cooking and burning wood and told me this can happen anytime, night or day. Oh! I thought. The other side said that there was a spirit man who keeps frightening their daughter who was only 17 years old. That confirmed it for me, I was glad to get out of there. Karla, my youngest daughter, asked me what we were going to do especially as I was still ill, getting over the treatment of cancer. She proposed that we should buy a house with a separate dwelling downstairs for Howie and me. Our luck was about to change at last as I slowly got better. We decided to find this dream house in West End, Southampton, Hampshire, and low and behold we found it. Karla phoned me up excitedly, "Mum, you are not going to believe this I've found the house, it's about 16 years old, the people who own it seem very nice but have to sell so went along to see it."

I was very sceptical after the last place but it had fantastic energy, as soon as I drove into the road the energy got stronger and when I walked through the front door the house hugged me with happiness. That was it, we are home. Plus, the separate door to the games room downstairs would be ideal for our dwelling, it was perfect. We got planning permission and a year later we renovated the downstairs. Everyone who comes to the house always says they love it and get happy feelings from the place. I can't wait to spend time here, I sleep well, I am happy and well. Lee is also doing well and living with Karla, so the house is always packed with people and I never have any black moments. I do my Reiki treatments as well in one of the rooms in the house and the energy is just flowing.

We have been living together in the main house

altogether, it has its moments but on the whole it's been fine, but this house's energy is gorgeous, we just feel so lucky at last!

Our builders are good, they are converting our dwelling downstairs, I still can't believe how happy energies are around even though there is builders' equipment everywhere, always happiness in this house. I was talking to the plasterer the other day and he said he's into all this type of energy thing and said how nice and balanced the energy is in the house, so there you are.

CHAPTER 5

Moved to Hampshire

We moved into our house on the 3rd December 2010 with three inches of snow on the ground but we didn't mind as I felt completely different moving into this home, I knew I was home at last and safe. It didn't take long to settle.

I soon joined a local health club and started taking Aqua and Pilate classes and quickly made friends, plus I was also getting fit. Yes, life was good and getting better. Slowly I met people at the club and they soon found out I did Reiki and started to book treatments with me.

My Pilates class teacher Hilary, I call her Hils, is a fabulous teacher, she is so kind to me; once, when I turned up with a wig on she laughed and told me to take it off and relax so I did. I also became friends with Maureen, we clicked immediately, she helped me and listened to me as I talked about my treatments and was a truly wonderful friend who I'm still friends with to this day. I still go over to her house and chat for hours. I met another friend at Pilates called Lynne, she was always chatting to Maureen, she was so nice and friendly, she would make me laugh; we were known as the three musketeers in class, the three of us always hanging around together.

Two lovely ladies from the Aqua class

befriended me, one was called Paula, a lovely smiley lady. She came to me for relaxation and wanted to know and experience Reiki. While Gerry was also such a lovely lady, we had a chat about how Reiki works and they both decided to book some treatments.

Gerry told me she has suffered from Fibromyalgia for years, so I told her about Peter and how Reiki relieved some of his suffering and hoped that Reiki would do the same for her. She came for her first treatment and it wasn't long before she started to relax into the treatment and begin enjoying; after a couple of treatments with her I suddenly saw this beautiful cat arrive in my Reiki room, it was a big grey cat with the most beautiful eyes I've ever seen and sat at the end of my massage table. I knew it was from the spirit world as this often happens in Reiki treatments as we bring them down, they like to take a look, they are so nosey! Sometimes they are connected to the person I am treating. The cat started to run all around the room, flying through the air, it was just amazing, I could hardly believe my eyes, I am so blessed to witness these things. The cat sat on Gerry's shoulder, gazing at her, which was lovely to watch. I thought there must be a connection somewhere, so I finished her treatment and then had a chat about what I found and also mentioned the cat. Sure enough Gerry knew who I was on about, "Oh that's Marcus, I adored him, I had him for 18 years, he was such a huge part of my life, I miss him very much."

Gerry was so touched to have her beloved cat come and say hello to her. Gerry continued coming to me for more treatments and Marcus always appeared, it was truly moving to witness.

As time went by more people heard about my Reiki treatments; I remember Alex, a nice chap who went to university with my youngest daughter Karla, asked if he could book some treatments with me. He always arrived on a Saturday morning as he worked all week. I thought he was purely coming for relaxation but I noticed some of his chakras were unbalanced and asked him what was going on in his life, he then told me he has panic attacks, sometimes they are so bad its effecting his social life. He came for nine treatments, his chakras were beginning to settle; on his last three treatments we had a visitor, a tall slender man stood by him with a hat which seemed to be from the 1940's, it was clearly his guide from the spirit world. I told Alex that he was being looked after and he just smiled in wonder. I told him to just come to me for occasional top-up treatments. Alex is firm friends with Karla and when I see him I always ask him how he is and he always says he hasn't had a panic attack since. Wow! Reiki can help so many people for so many different reasons; as Reiki practitioner we never say to someone that we can heal, but for some reason it just finds a way of helping the person and never ceases to amaze me. If you are tired, busy, stressed out or just want some time to yourself, then a Reiki treatment is for you! Some of the benefits of a Reiki treatment include: -

Balancing the body's energies and increasing your own energy levels. Promoting a state of calm and relaxation which helps to "re-set" you. Improving your physical, mental, emotional and spiritual state.

We live in such a beautiful place, we have the River Parks on the River Itchen, swans, so much greenery, a large putting green, birds, ducks, we have kingfishers and Otters, although I've never seen one, as well as trout. It's such a great place to go for a walk, which I regularly do. One day on my regular walk on the river bank I met this lady who I started to talk to, she looked tired, in pain, she was with her husband and had two beautiful dogs, which was the topic of conversation. As we were walking along together I noticed she was walking "like a duck" with a stick, she was telling me she had a hip replacement a few months ago and didn't feel well. So I told her about Reiki, she told me she had a Reiki with someone and it was marvellous but had lost touch with her. I told her to come and see me as I do Reiki treatments. She agreed. We exchanged phone numbers. When I phoned her she was so pleased to hear from me. She was a lot younger than I thought when I asked her how old she was, I made a promise we would get together very soon and get started with her Reiki treatments. Sure enough the day arrived and she booked an appointment to come for her treatment. I was getting really excited to treat and help Danae, she was my very first client when we moved to Southampton. When I greeted her the first thing I smelt was smoke on her, it was horrible, it was on her clothes and her hair. I asked her if she smoked and she confirmed she did, so I told her that Reiki treatments help you to kick bad habits. She told me she smoked because it helped with her pain, but I told her that Reiki would help her relax without smoking. As the months went by Danae eventually said to me one day that she had given up smoking, and to this day, one year and two months later, she still hasn't had a cigarette. It made me so happy that she listened to me, plus her wallet is better these days too! As we were progressing with Danae I felt great heat in her hip, the hip she had surgery on, it got better with time, but she was still not walking properly so I told her to have a check- up at the hospital because with the amount of treatments she had had by now it should be much better than it is. When she went to the hospital the x-ray showed up that they had put the wrong size in her hip and admitted their mistake, she is now waiting to have it rectified. Although Danae is still in pain, she is more positive and brighter and she looks 10 years younger. She still comes to me for Reiki treatments as she says she loves to come as she loves the peace and relaxation that Reiki gives her. This just proves that Reiki can be used for so many things.

Danae owned a little chihuahua called Joey, he was such a sweet little thing, but I felt his pain in his neck. Danae asked me to help him and I did. This is a photo of Joey and a short testimonial.

When we got Joey at five months old, he had an issue with his neck. Pretty much every couple of days he would get a "crick" in it and get stuck and cry out. This went on for some time, I mentioned this to Anne during one of my Reiki sessions and she suggested bringing him to see her. I took him and she made him calm, he actually dozed off in my arms as she treated him, he was so still. She felt his neck was warm and she could feel the painful parts. Anne treated him for quite some time and he was relaxed and perfectly calm as she gave him Reiki.

From that day on I can honestly say the pain has never returned.

He is now nine years old, happy and healthy, and I will be forever grateful to Anne for helping him that day.

Hugs. Joey ....

CHAPTER 6

Amazing Experiences

Sonya, a lady I met at my Aqua class who I love to talk to, she is so giggly when she laughs, she has a smashing energy, asked me if she could book some treatments with me, she comes every Tuesday. She was complaining of pain on the left side of her back; it did seem painful, she looked ill, poor lady. I quickly got to work on her back, it took a few treatments to ease her pain but we got there in the end. One day, while doing her treatment, I was at her feet and looked up saw a white feathery angel above her head, I told Sonya about this afterwards and she told me that she thought this angel was protecting her. Sonya recommended me to her best friends, which was lovely; one of her friends who came to see me was a gentlemen called Roy, he was an absolute joy to work with, but he clearly wasn't well, he suffered from a prolapse in his spine, he was in dreadful pain. When he arrived for his treatment he was really slouched and clearly in great pain with his back. I told him to hop up, so to speak, on my couch, and then we will begin. But I always ask my clients to wash their hands and then get onto my Reiki table, with candles burning, and beautiful healing music playing and then away we go! The third time Roy came to see me I experienced great heat from his shoulder, it seemed to last for about ten minutes, my hands became very sweaty but I stayed in this position until it cooled. thought to myself what a nasty blockage; the next time he came it was much better so I was so pleased I had cleared it, or Reiki had. He clearly enjoyed the treatments and booked to come weekly for a while until his back began improving. He was also having treatment from a sports physio, and now he only comes for top ups. I always look forward to seeing him, he is a keen rower and has his own boat, so he was grateful to Reiki for helping him and his physio, he can also sail again now and enjoys life without pain. Oh, and he walks much straighter too!

I always feel blessed with all my clients, who first come to me with closed hearts and it is so lovely to see them blossom like a beautiful Orchid flower, fully open in the heart chakra. The true meaning of Love and Light within us all.

When life seems hopeless and you feel you can't help yourself turn to Reiki it really does help because it's a natural healing with everyone who uses it. It is so true. If it is physical or emotional it helps to balance you to get to grips with life. If you have house plants and they look tired give them some energy I do this often by holding my hands by the side of the plant and breath in and out pure energy if you are Reiki trained give them a power symbol and hold the position for 10 minutes the plant will love it.

I always bless my food before I eat it! I think it tastes better as well, when I have a drink of water or a cheeky glass of wine or a good old cuppa I do the same.

CHAPTER 7

Time Out

After four months or so and loads of stress with the building conversion on our new home I have started to return to writing, at first, I couldn't think what to write, my mind went blank, never mind trying to write with builders about (we all know the upheaval it causes having builders in your home). It's bad enough when they are building but then it's done and dusted and we can all get moved in and start to return to normal. WRONG. We had a leak and damp patches in our bedroom, and with the rain we have had this year it really was apparent there was a problem. We reported it but for a few months nothing was done, so eventually I contacted the Council surveyor to see if he could help, he was lovely and helpful but said as the property had been signed off there was not much he could do and suggested we contact our builders again. We were lucky they came back and repaired it, we have had plenty of rain since and all is dry so far.

Thank heavens for Reiki, as it really has been a really stressful time for me and my family, but the days have been much happier because of my Reiki. So, here I am writing again after a long break, and with all the problems behind us we can enjoy our lives once more. That's why I believe in Reiki so much for me, my family, my clients, my animals, trees, plants, every living thing in our universe.

Anything that has energy is worth doing a Reiki on. Don't laugh, when my laptop started playing up I gave it some Reiki and guess what, it worked!

One time, when I went to visit my daughter Sarah, who now lives in Yorkshire, we were walking through a forest of trees and I said to Sarah, "Let's feel the energy of each tree," which we did. People walking by must have thought we were crackers hugging the trees but we didn't care, we were having fun! Each tree felt different, some had earthy energy, some had lighter energies. I must tell you when we go on our local walks by the River Itchen, you will always find me hugging a tree, I love it! Try it for yourself, they give back some wonderful energy which will recharge you; trees have been with us for years, they have so much history which can be passed on. Also, when you touch a tree you are giving the tree your energy and it's such a treat when you receive the trees energy as well, it is a shared thing. Try it you'll enjoy it!

Trees have been around for thousands of years in parks, forests, coastal areas they are so good for our environment, so give them a little extra help as they give to us.

Be a tree hugger you will be amazed how they like it and give back to you.

CHAPTER 8

Back to Writing

It's time to get my thoughts together of all the wonderful experiences that I would love to share with you. I have so many thoughts buried in my brain it's time to release them onto paper.

Time waits for no man. That is so true. Remember me talking about Danae earlier on, she had a hip replacement and came to me for a long time but I wasn't satisfied with her progress and told her to go to the hospital to get things checked out, she did and the day finally arrived where they would redo her hip operation. She came for a Reiki session one week before the operation to calm her and to lap up the Reiki energy. I promised to visit her in hospital after her operation, which I did; she found it hard to cope with hospital food so each day I brought her some food, sandwiches, soup, fruit, but she wasn't feeling too well after her operation and went downhill. I started to worry, but immediately thought of Reiki and began to give her a Reiki treatment right there on the hospital bed; the other patients were looking at what I was doing, so in the end I had to draw the curtains, but it was great fun! I visited Danae most days and each day Danae began to feel better. She was very brave and I'm sure that her Reiki sessions helped her. Once she was out of hospital it was a slow road to recovery but her family and friends were wonderful. She is having physio at the hospital and is also having her Reiki sessions with me; she's driving her car again and is nearly back to her normal bubbly self. Bless her!

When I went to my health club for my Aqua class and one of my friends, Margaret, appeared to be hanging around in the dressing room and seemed as though she wanted to talk to me. She is a very interesting lady, she's a Buddhist and goes to Tibet and India regularly; the stories of her visits are amazing, she once told me that there is a beautiful family that adopted Margaret and look after her when she stays with them. Anyway, as I was saying, Margaret wanted to talk to me about her knees and how they are a bit sore/stiff when she gets up or bending. So I said I would do a quick Reiki treatment on her, she sat down and I laid my hands on her knees, there seemed to be a bit of tingling in her left knee and a little in her right. I couldn't find any physical problem or cold blockages in her knees but it seemed as though she was holding some kind of resentment of some kind. She then went on to explain that when she was last on holiday there were some issues she couldn't resolve. She was so grateful and I assured her that she would be okay and to not worry about her issues. We went into the lounge in our club and chatted further, I held her hand and gave her a Reiki goodbye and wished her well. Margaret asked me for a Reiki session when she returns from India. I look forward to seeing her again and hearing about all her travels.

The other day I bent over to put my washing in

the machine, as I bent over the most dreadful pain spread across my sacrum, it was like a nerve pain, it was an unimaginable pain, I was doubled over frightened to move; never in my life have I experienced such pain. For a split second I panicked, I didn't know what to do, then Reiki came to me, I placed both hands on my back, where the pain was, I left my hands there for at least 10 minutes, perhaps it was longer, then somehow I straightened up and suddenly the pain was gone. I started to walk a few steps and couldn't believe that there was no pain (laugh if you may, I did afterwards, I felt stupid bent over like a puppet on a string). I went to Pilates about an hour later and told my instructor Hilary, she just smiled and couldn't believe I had healed myself. I then told my dear friend Maureen who told me I have a gift. To this day I haven't had a tingle of pain. Reiki is for everyone, it's the most wonderful First Aid tool.

Talking about my Pilates class, I was

approached by a very elegant lady once asked me if Reiki could help her, she explained that she had spent a lot of money trying different healing methods without success. I felt sorry and sad for her as she badly needed my help. I told her to come and see me and I would give her a free session so she could become comfortable with the rhythm of Reiki's, as it was clear she needed to relax. She also told me that her father was not kind to her when she was a child and throughout her adult life she worries constantly: this is a very common complaint. I told her that I was a worrier many years ago and that Reiki changed my life. When you worry it affects everything you do, your life is taken over you feel tired, weary, with loads on your shoulders. When you get rid of the worry life opens up like a beautiful flower, like a lovely orchid, with its beautiful petals open wide. As you read this, I can honestly say to you I am the happiest person on the planet, truly I am, obviously I have days where something might go wrong, but it doesn't weigh me down like it used to, I am so grateful that I trained in Reiki.

CHAPTER 9

Moments to Cherish

Life has settled down now, a few years have passed and there are many more memories I wish to share with you. When I met Andrea, my Reiki Master, I thought she was incredibly interesting, once she organised a trip to Stone Henge where we were allowed to stand in the circle of the stones, it felt amazing, whilst she performed a ceremony welcoming us all. I couldn't resist picking a few strands of grass from the circle which I've kept to this day.

I felt I could trust Andrea, which is what Reiki is all about. We are all different, aren't we? I connected with Andrea wholeheartedly so I decided it was time to learn the Master level of Reiki. There was about six of us in the class who were taking the Master's degree over a two-day course. I must add that it takes time an entire year or so to qualify from one level to the next, to let your bodies energies settle, with the last bit being the two days course with the qualification on the second day. The other Reiki Masters that took the qualification with me were very special people, they were so pure in heart and I realised I was as well. I connected with a beautiful lady called Donna, she is a reflexologist at the hospital and wanted to expand her skills. We keep in touch to this day, with our modern technology. This was in 2014 and remember the qualification day so well. I actually cried with happiness to receive my Masters certificate, I was so overwhelmed by the day, I think we were all blown away by it. I felt such a blessed and powerful energy to achieve this and be able to help others. My youngest daughter Karla and her husband Lee went for a holiday to Cornwall and when they came back they handed me a beautiful Amethyst as a present for achieving my Masters. This made me want to learn about crystals as they have energies of their own. I placed them in my room to help with the energy and when I do Reiki it helps absorb the negative energy and give off positive energy and calm the room. I've learnt more about crystals that they are pretty to look at and to wear; I have a Super 7 crystal which I wear around my neck, it's supposed to protect all your chakras. If you hold the crystal up to the light you can actually see all the colours of our chakras, that's why they call the stone Super 7. It's supposed to protect the chakras of the person who is fortunate enough to wear and own one.

I started to collect crystals from different countries around the world. I started looking in market places an incredible find, tumble stones you can display them in pretty dishes like the one my daughter Karla brought back from France and filled it up with several stones I placed them in my bathroom, bedroom, kitchen and lounge. Many years ago I was given a rose quartz from a dear friend Jenny who died a few years ago. I love Rose quartz one where you can burn a tee light in. A pretty glow of pink fills the room. Clear quartz is a finding stone to me, I lost an earring I dropped the clear quartz by my bedside table it rolled underneath my bed when I pushed the bed back I couldn't believe it, there was my earring next to the clear quartz lovely little stone that finds things. Another gift I received recently from Barbara she gave me a silver necklace with a Howlite stones, pretty blue stones they use to make jewellery it seems to have a calming effect when you wear it. I bought myself a large Selenite crystal I have placed it in my kitchen to keep me calm whilst writing my book hopefully remembering to write everything. Selenite brings Good Luck also mystical properties.

In 2016 I decided to embark on the Holy Fire 11, a new energy, which would provide me with a lovely gentle energy which was powerful, and would make my Reiki sessions much easier. I can now teach all levels of Reiki.

I was contacted by Andrea to update my Reiki skills energy to the Holy Fire 111, which I was so excited about, it meant I would be able to use Reiki treatments and teach in this energy, so I contacted the International Center for Reiki Training, Holy Fire 111 Reiki Ryoho, to be certified and receive the upgrade along with the necessary instruction and training. It was on the 11th January 2019 I received this upgrade. I was so excited and proud to use these new skills.

To explain placements to others, we simply say that they are how attunements are given in Holy Fire Reiki.

So, this is a new way of teaching and giving Reiki placements much easier than before (even I can do it) all my teaching now is in the new energy.

I had just received my Holy Fire 111 upgrade when I met a lady Natasha chatting with her telling her about Reiki and how it works she was very interested in knowing more about it.

A nurse from Southampton hospital, on one of my walks down the Riverside, I told her about Reiki and how it helped others. She wanted to train with me for Reiki 1 and 11 and is now herself qualified. I am very proud of her as she has progressed further in her career too, Reiki helped her to move forward and achieve what she really wanted to do.

I would also love to tell you about my dear

friend Barbara, but her friends call her Babs! I met Babs a few years ago through my daughter's partner who was in business in Bournemouth. We hit it off straight away, she's lively and a bit nutty, just like me. Her energies are so grounded, she is such a special, kind, loving person and it is always lovely to spend time with her. She once asked me if she could have a Reiki session, of course I said yes. I travelled to her beautiful house in Bournemouth put up my couch, music and candles and away we went. The whole room was filled with love just as I expected it to be. Babs relaxed into the session nicely and thanked me for the session. A few years later Babs gave me a present a gold Buddha which I still have, I love it as it always reminds me of our beautiful friendship.

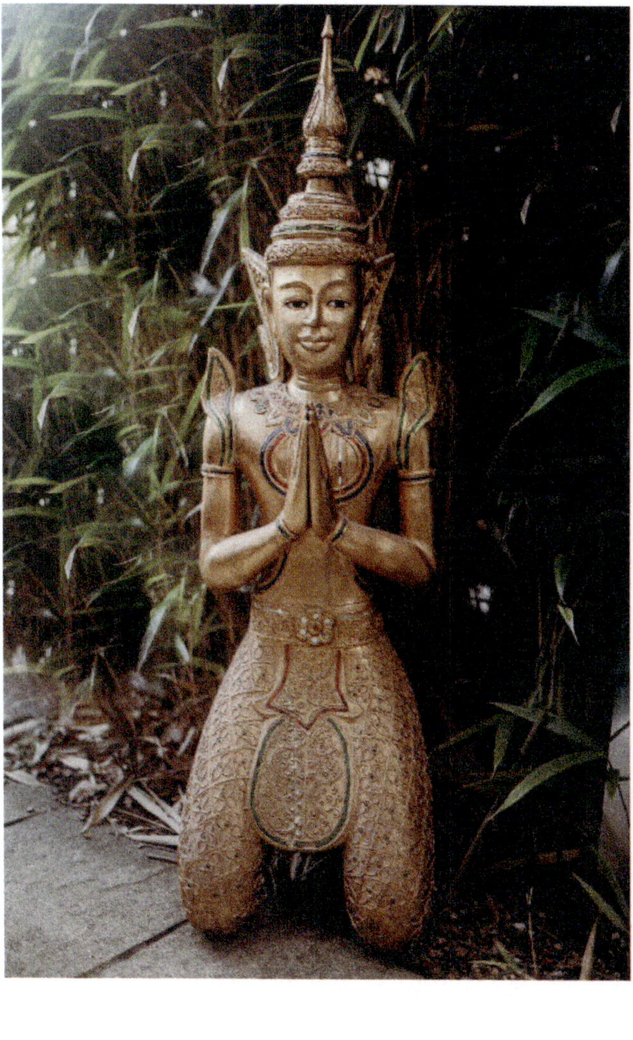

Around about the same time I met a lady from my club called Lin, she was unrelaxed but had really lovely energies. We chatted in the garden outside pool area of the club, then it suddenly dawned on me how she could benefit from a Reiki treatment. She came and loved them, slowly she got better, all her anxiety began to leave her and she was starting to feel happy again. She won't mind me mentioning this but one Reiki session was very intense, with the curtains drawn, the most intense bright light came through the windows, I had never seen anything like it before, it was like a ball of bright light covering the whole of my lounge area. I stopped the Reiki session as I was taken aback, I checked on Lin, "Are you okay?"

"Oh yes," she said, "it is Gloria come to say hello to me. She sadly passed away a few years back." Lin and Gloria were very close, it was such a shock when she died.

Lin told her husband about the Reiki session and told him how it might help his back as he was in terrible pain. So, I visited their home and put my hands on Colin's sacrum, he told me he could feel the heat and said he would come and have a Reiki session. He did and it made such a difference to him. When he was in the hospital the doctor told him he would need further treatment, possibly an operation. So, Colin came to me for another Reiki session and said he wasn't keen on more treatment or an operation. During my training I have learnt about a technique that can relieve back imbalances, so I asked him if he would like me to have a go.

"Yes please," he said, "why not give it a try."

So, the day arrived, Colin trusted me, which was nice, and I told him not to worry and we got going on the technique for his back. A few days later when he came back he seemed okay and free from pain. They were both so pleased with the Reiki treatment that their daughter Amanda came for a relaxation session a few times, such a pretty tall girl, it's always wonderful to see her and she also seems to enjoy her Reiki's.

Lin and Colin have a wonderful life in Spain, they decided to retire there. They invited me and my husband to their beautiful villa, we had a wonderful time with them. While I was there I asked Colin, "How's the back?"

"Yep, okay, no problems." With a cheeky smile on his face.

I'm always on WhatsApp to Lin, I'm so happy they have found happiness in Spain.

I must point out our Reiki sessions given is for the purpose of stress reduction, and relaxation. A Reiki session is not a substitute for medical, or psychological diagnosis, and treatment. Reiki practitioners do not diagnose conditions, nor do they prescribe, perform medical treatment, nor prescribe substances, nor interfere with the treatment of a licensed medical professional.

I love hearing about success stories in Reiki, but mustn't be confused with the medical profession. Although in my opinion Reiki helps tremendously in many ways. Like the testimonials I have received and put in my book.

Testimonial from Lin and Colin

My wife Linda has been going to Anne for Reiki sessions over a six-year period, during which time she has become a very good friend of ours. I was having a lot of pain in my lower back and visited my GP and the hospital for an MRI scan.

The hospital did an MRI scan and told me I had two trapped nerves at the base of my spine, I was offered injections to relieve the pain but was told that they wouldn't last very long. The alternative was back surgery which I thought would be too invasive. I tried a chiropractor and acupuncture. Anne suggested that I should try some Reiki treatments, which really helped to relax me and made me feel much better. Then in one of my visits Anne suggested something specialized and asked whether I would be willing to give it ago. I agreed and fully trusted her. I could feel a warmth and a sense of healing.

Throughout the treatment and I felt refreshed, enlightened and after several sessions I was pain free. I would recommend the healing power of Reiki and Anne is a very professional and well-established teacher and healer in her field.

Testimonial from Lin 4th May 2022

Personally, I found Reiki not only helps with the physical side of our bodies but there seems to be a great power to help our mental state of mind, it relieves stress and tension and relaxes the body in each of these forms. I found that Reiki relieved some of the personal anxieties that I had been holding onto for a number of years which Anne picked up on when I first met her. I think that she was drawn to me partly for that reason. I feel that she has a great gift of being able to connect with people that need her skills and knowledge. Not only did Reiki relieve my stress levels but it also made me feel more relaxed, energised and encouraged me to lose the weight I had been struggling with for so long and lead me to live a much healthier lifestyle. It proves that if your mind is not right and you are under a lot of stress it can affect your whole body. So having regular Reiki sessions can be very beneficial for us………

I was in touch with a Reiki Master, Anne Gelder, at one of our conventions back in 2007, she sent me a Christmas card in 2008, I was very touched I wanted to put this in my book

> The Love which Reiki imparts
> truly gladdens all our hearts
> the purest light which connects
> to cherish and share a most precious gift.
>
> Anne Gelder 16/12/2008

Thank you, Anne, for your most beautiful poem.

What a great way to finish my book

Thank you to everyone who has supported me in writing my book, maybe it will inspire some of you to learn Reiki. Enjoy reading my story on my Reiki journey.

My love goes to my family, my beautiful grandchildren whom I love unconditionally, Annabella, Thea and Aston.

Reiki Light and love to you all. Hugs Anne xx
Namaste